D0560559

SLOTH

A DICTIONARY FOR THE LAZY

JENNIFER M. WOOD

Aadamsmedia
Avon, Massachusetts

Published by
Adams Media, a division of F+W Media, Inc.
57 Littlefield Street, Avon, MA 02322. U.S.A.
www.adamsmedia.com

ISBN 10: 1-4405-2806-3
ISBN 13: 978-1-4405-2806-4
eISBN 10: 1-4405-2835-7
eISBN 13: 978-1-4405-2835-4

Printed in the United States of America.

10   9   8   7   6   5   4   3   2   1

Library of Congress Cataloging-in-Publication Data
is available from the publisher.

This publication is designed to provide accurate and authoritative
information with regard to the subject matter covered. It is sold
with the understanding that the publisher is not engaged in
rendering legal, accounting, or other professional advice. If legal
advice or other expert assistance is required, the services of a
competent professional person should be sought.
　　　　—From a *Declaration of Principles* jointly adopted
　　　　by a Committee of the American Bar Association
　　　　and a Committee of Publishers and Associations

Many of the designations used by manufacturers and sellers to
distinguish their product are claimed as trademarks. Where
those designations appear in this book and Adams Media was
aware of a trademark claim, the designations have been printed
with initial capital letters.

Illustration © clipart.com

This book is available at quantity discounts for bulk purchases.
For information, please call 1-800-289-0963.

An Introduction to
Sloth

sloth
(*slawth*)
NOUN: Consistent aversion to exertion.

North winds set Odysseus off-course landing him on the island of the Lotus Eaters. Tempted by the native tribe's beautiful bounty of delicious flowers, the men who indulged lost their fervor to venture on. Lethargy enwrapped the sailors as the allure of the Lotus Eaters' indolence subdued any want to return home. Similar to the power of the island people's plant, the strength of sloth is in the sin's subtle ability to make one disregard their responsibilities, dissolve any resolve to achieve, and laze about without worry. Clear the cloudiness of languor by leafing through the dictionary that defines the idlest of vices.

A

abeyance

(*uh-BEH-uhns*)

NOUN: Being in a state of temporary inactivity. The word is often preceded by "in" or "into."

abjure

(*ab-JUR*)

VERB: To avoid or abstain from; to recant or renounce, possibly under oath.

abortive

(*ah-BAWR-tiv*)

ADJECTIVE: Failing to come to completion.

Her pre-emptively ABORTIVE nature left remnants of projects in progress strewn about the house.

abstain

(*ab-STAYN*)

VERB: To refrain from doing something desirable; often used in relation to alcohol consumption or sexual activity.

accumbent

(*uh-KUHM-buhnt*)

ADJECTIVE: In a reclined position; recumbent.

acedia
(*uh-SEE-dee-uh*)
NOUN: A state of indifference, especially in relation to spiritual or religious matters.

aimless
(*EYM-lis*)
ADJECTIVE: Without a clear direction; purposeless.

aloof
(*uh-LOOF*)
ADJECTIVE: Disinterested or indifferent.

amble
(*am-BUHL*)
VERB: To move at a slow pace; meander.

The old man would AMBLE aimlessly between the couch and the bed a few times a day.

apathetic
(*ap-uh-THET-ik*)
ADJECTIVE: Uncaring or uninterested.

aposiopesis
(*ap-uh-sy-uh-PEE-sis*)
NOUN: Stopping talking in the midst of a sentence, either because you physically cannot or mentally do not want to; an unfinished thought.

I don't think necessity is

the mother of invention.

Invention, in my opinion,

arises directly from idleness,

possibly also from laziness.

To save oneself trouble.

—AGATHA CHRISTIE

ardorless

(*AHR-der-lis*)

ADJECTIVE: Without warmth or passion; lack of enthusiasm.

> *She was so ARDORLESS that her face remained cold and bored, even when holding her newborn daughter.*

B

backside
(*BAK-syd*)
NOUN: Buttocks; rearend.

backrest
(*BAK-rest*)
NOUN: A support or rest for one's back.

bagatelle
(*bag-uh-tel*)
NOUN: A thing of little importance; a very easy task.

> *Her day is filled with many small and meaningless activities; each BAGATELLE demanding very little of her attention.*

baked
(*BAY-kt*)
ADJECTIVE: Intoxicated to the point of lethargy.

balk
(*bawk*)
VERB: To stop oneself from moving forward; to hesitate from accomplishing a goal.

Sloth and silence

are a fool's virtues.

—BENJAMIN FRANKLIN

barnacle

(*BAHR-nuh-kuhl*)

NOUN: Something that attaches itself to something else in a dogged manner; a crustacean that gloms onto the bottom of a boat.

beachcomber

(*BEECH-koh-mer*)

NOUN: Literally, a person who combs the beach looking for valuables that others may have left behind.

beck

(*bek*)

NOUN: A signal or gesture to summon or direct someone.

bed

(*bed*)

NOUN: A piece of furniture upon which one sleeps or rests.

bedfast

(*BED-fast*)

ADJECTIVE: Restricted to one's bed.

bedroom

(*BED-room*)

NOUN: A room intended for sleeping.

boondoggle

(*BOON-dog-hul*)

NOUN: An activity that is wasteful or pointless but gives the appearance of having value. When used as a verb, it can mean to deceive or to engage in an activity of little value.

bootless

(*BOOT-lis*)

ADJECTIVE: Failing to achieve result or advantage; fruitless.

> *All of our BOOTLESS searching felt like a waste, yet we continued looking for the legendary document.*

bum

(*buhm*)

NOUN: A slacker; the word is often used (in a disparaging manner) in reference to homeless people.

bystander

(*BY-stan-der*)

NOUN: One who observes an activity but does not get involved in it.

C

careless

(*KAYR-lis*)

ADJECTIVE: Without care or concern; negligent.

catnap

(*KAT-nap*)

NOUN: A quick nap; as a verb, it's the act of taking a quick nap.

cavalier

(*KAV-uh-leer*)

ADJECTIVE: Showing a lack of concern for an otherwise important person or thing; disdainful.

> *He was CAVALIER regarding the wedding; while his future bride planned fervidly and glowed with excitement, he stared ahead, unblinking.*

cessation

(*se-SAY-shuhn*)

NOUN: A stoppage, often permanently; termination.

chill

(*chil*)

VERB: Traditionally referring to a feeling of coldness, it's also slang for the act of relaxing; to hang out.

Ambition is a poor excuse

for not having sense enough

to be lazy.

—Edgar Bergen

clock-watcher
(*klok-WOCH-er*)
NOUN: Originally used to refer to an apathetic employee who spends his or her day watching the clock for when it's time to go home, the phrase can be used to describe anyone with a clear lack of interest in an activity.

comatose
(*KOHM-muh-tohs*)
ADJECTIVE: In addition to being used in a medical setting to characterize someone in a coma, it can also be used to describe a lack of energy or awareness.

conciliatory
(*kohn-SIL-ee-uh-tawr-ee*)
ADJECTIVE: Describes someone or thing that is pacifying or willing to compromise to keep peace.

> *With his CONCILIATORY payment in hand, he promised to be on his best behavior for the rest of the event.*

costive
(*KAW-stiv*)
ADJECTIVE: Traditionally refers to constipation of anything that causes constipation but is also used to describe slow or listless people and things.

couch

(*kouch*)

VERB: As a noun, it's a piece of furniture; as a verb, it can mean to lie down or lay something down in order to rest.

couch potato

(*kouch puh-TAY-toh*)

NOUN: An inactive person who spends all of his or her time on the couch, watching TV or being otherwise entertained from a sedentary position.

couchant

(*KOU-chuhnt*)

ADJECTIVE: Lying down but with a raised head.

It is extremely difficult to dine COUCHANT, but Adele was so lazy and so willing to sit up that she eventually found a way.

cunctation

(*kohngk-TAY-shuhn*)

NOUN: A hesitation or delay.

D

dabbler

(*DAB-ler*)

NOUN: One who participates in an event or interest on a superficial level only; dilettante.

He was a DABBLER in music and never learned to play any instrument particularly well.

dally

(*DAL-ee*)

VERB: To waste time or loiter; to act in a playful manner.

dawdle

(*DAWD-l*)

VERB: To loiter; to waste time unnecessarily.

deadness

(*DED-nis*)

NOUN: A lack of inactivity so as to appear to be without life; numbness; extreme exhaustion.

deferral

(*dih-FUR-uhl*)

NOUN: The act of putting something off.

derelict

(*DER-uh-likt*)

ADJECTIVE: Neglectful or negligent of one's responsibilities; it can also be used as a noun in reference to such a person or to someone who has no home, job, or family.

> *The DERELICT mother often forgot to buy milk for the children or put them to bed on time.*

dereliction

(*der-uh-LIK-shuhn*)

NOUN: To purposefully and knowingly neglect one's responsibilities.

desist

(*dih-ZIST*)

VERB: To stop or cease.

desk-bound

(*DESK-bound*)

ADJECTIVE: Work that involves a lot of sitting or does not allow for one to leave his or her desk.

desultory

(*DES-uhl-tawr-ee*)

ADJECTIVE: Aimless of unfocused; lacking any organization or regularity.

Idleness is not

doing nothing.

Idleness is being free

to do anything.

—FLOYD DELL

detachment

(*dih-TACH-muhnt*)

NOUN: Aloofness or disconnection, either physically or emotionally.

devoid

(*dih-VOID*)

ADJECTIVE: Lacking completely; existing without.

Her face was DEVOID of any emotion; it was difficult to know exactly what she was feeling, if anything.

diddle-daddle

(*DID-l-dad-l*)

VERB: To dawdle or loiter; dilly-dally.

dilatory

(*DIL-uh-tawr-ee*)

ADJECTIVE: Putting something off; being a procrastinator.

dilly-dally

(*DIL-ee-dal-ee*)

VERB: To waste time or dawdle; to loiter.

directionless

(*dih-REK-shuhn-lis*)

ADJECTIVE: Without direction or clear purpose.

He was DIRECTIONLESS in college and never chose anything to study specifically.

disinterested

(*dis-IN-tuh-res-tid*)

ADJECTIVE: Showing a lack of interest or concern.

dispassionate

(*dis-PASH-uh-nit*)

ADJECTIVE: A lack of passion or emotion toward something; unbiased.

do-nothing

(*DOO-nuhth-ing*)

NOUN: Someone who is lazy; a person who literally chooses to "do nothing."

dodger

(*DOJ-er*)

NOUN: One who avoids his or her responsibilities; shirker.

dolittle

(*DOO-lit-l*)

NOUN: Literally, one who does little; do-nothing.

doodle

(*DOOD-l*)

VERB: To take part in an inconsequential activity; to draw something in an unplanned, absent-minded manner.

dormant

(*DAWR-muhnt*)

ADJECTIVE: Being in a state of inactivity.

For years she was DORMANT, reclining on the couch for hours each day, rising only when necessary and quickly lying back down again.

dozy

(*DOH-zee*)

ADJECTIVE: Sleepy or drowsy.

dreaminess

(*DREE-mee-nis*)

NOUN: A dreamlike state or pensiveness; a perfectly pleasurable dreamlike state.

drifter

(*DRIF-ter*)

NOUN: One who is constantly moving from place to place—home, job, etc.—without any clear path or goal.

drone

(*drohn*)

NOUN: One who does not want to work or help in any way; a loafer. As a verb, it means to talk excessively in a very monotone, boring manner.

droop

(*droop*)

VERB: To sag or hang down; to become disheartened.

dropout

(*DROP-out*)

VERB: Abandoning something before completion, including an educational program or society; as a noun, it defines one who abandons something before completion.

dross

(*draws*)

NOUN: Something that is useless or of low quality; rubbish.

How did you spend money on such DROSS when you know it will just fall apart in a few days?

drowse

(*drouz*)

VERB: Being midway between sleep and wakefulness.

drowsy

(*DROU-zee*)

ADJECTIVE: Sleepy, tired; sluggish.

E

effete

(*ih-FEET*)

ADJECTIVE: Devoid of energy or vivacity; no longer able to produce.

emotionless

(*ih-MOH-shuhn-lis*)

ADJECTIVE: Lacking any emotion or passion, particularly in a situation where it would be expected or called for.

enervate

(*EN-er-vayt*)

VERB: To weaken one's physical, psychological, or moral strength or vibrance; debilitate.

> *To spend so much time resting would ENERVATE anyone, making it nearly impossible to resume a normal life.*

ennui

(*ahn-WEE*)

NOUN: From the French word for apathy or boredom, *ennui* is a feeling of boredom and discontent with life.

ergophobia

(*ER-goh-foh-bee-uh*)

NOUN: Fear of work.

Sloth is of all the passions

the most powerful . . .

—SAMUEL BECKETT

eschew

(*es-CHOO*)

VERB: To abstain from or avoid.

evade

(*ih-VAYD*)

VERB: To use one's ingenuity to avoid or escape something; elude.

He had a knack for being able to EVADE any kind of responsibility or obligation, leaving all of his spare time for himself.

exanimate

(*eg-ZAN-uh-mit*)

ADJECTIVE: Without life or expression; lifeless.

exhaust

(*ig-ZAWST*)

VERB: To deplete all of something; the word could refer to one's energy level or a resource such as food.

F

failing
(*FAY-ling*)
NOUN: A failure or shortcoming.

fainéant
(*FAY-nee-uhnt*)
NOUN: A French term for a lazy person or slacker. Can also be used as an adjective to describe such a person.

fatigue
(*fuh-TEEG*)
NOUN: Extreme exhaustion, usually as a result of overexertion. As a verb it means to cause extreme exhaustion.

feeble
(*FEE-buhl*)
ADJECTIVE: Physically or mentally weak.

feckless
(*FEK-lis*)
ADJECTIVE: Lacking any sense of responsibility or ambition.

> *Your son is so FECKLESS that he will probably never seek a job or move out of your home.*

fiddle

(*FID-l*)

VERB: To waste time; to move one's hands or fingers in a nervous manner; as a noun it's a stringed musical instrument in the same family as the violin or to play that instrument.

fixed

(*fikst*)

ADJECTIVE: Stationary; as a verb it means to put something into order or to prearrange the outcome of something that should be random (as in fixing a horse race).

flop

(*flop*)

VERB: To plop down on something in a careless, tired fashion; informally, it can mean to stay at someone's house—to crash; to fail; to change one's mind rather unexpectedly.

Once she arrived home, she would FLOP onto the couch and wait for dinner to be brought to her.

Idleness and lack of

occupation tend—nay are

dragged—towards evil.

—HIPPOCRATES

foot-dragger

(*foot-DRAG-er*)

NOUN: Literally, one who drags his or her feet in order to do anything; idler.

footle

(*FOOT-l*)

VERB: To behave foolishly; to waste time, usually used with "about" or "around."

freeloader

(*FREE-lohd-er*)

NOUN: One who relies on others for his or her basic needs, including food and shelter, without the intention of paying them back.

frowzy

(*FROU-zee*)

ADJECTIVE: Shabby or unkempt

> *The FROWZY girl hadn't combed her hair in days; her dress was shabby and her shoes were untied.*

fruitless

(*FROOT-lis*)

ADJECTIVE: Unproductive; an activity or thing that produces no results.

futile

(*FYOOT-tyl*)

ADJECTIVE: Pointless; ineffective.

futz

(*fuhts*)

VERB: To waste in an aimless or lazy manner.

> *It was not unlike him to FUTZ about the house with meaningless projects when there was work to be done.*

G

gadabout

(*GAD-uh-bout*)

NOUN: One who wanders around without purpose, often in the pursuit of something pleasurable.

> *Philip was such a GADABOUT; roaming town to town looking for the best pub and most beautiful women in each new place.*

gainless

(*GAYN-lis*)

ADJECTIVE: Without profit or results.

gape

(*gayp*)

VERB: To widely open one's mouth due to sleepiness; yawn.

gauche

(*gohsh*)

ADJECTIVE: Lacking the wherewithal to behave properly in social situations.

gestate

(*JES-tayt*)

VERB: To generate and develop slowly.

Failure is not the only

punishment for laziness;

there is also

the success of others.

—JULES RENARD

give up
(*giv uhp*)
VERB: To stop putting forth an effort; to admit defeat.

glacial
(*GLAY-shuhl*)
ADJECTIVE: Characterized by the pace of a glacier's movement; slow.

glaze (over)
(*glayz OH-ver*)
VERB: To become glassy or lacking expression, usually out of boredom.

glob
(*glob*)
NOUN: A lump of a moldable substance.

gluteus
(*GLOO-tee-uhs*)
NOUN: Any of the muscles of the buttocks.

goalless
(*gohl-lis*)
ADJECTIVE: Without goals; aimless.

goldbrick
(*GOHLD-brik*)
NOUN: A shirker; a worthless thing that appears valuable.

good-for-nothing
(*GOOD-fer-nuhth-ing*)
NOUN: Self-explanatorily, a person who does not bring value to any situation. Can also be used as an adjective to describe a worthless person.

goof-off
(*GOOF-awf*)
NOUN: Can be used as a noun or adjective in reference to a person who does not channel his or her energy toward any worthwhile endeavor; a slacker.

groggy
(*GROG-ee*)
ADJECTIVE: Dazed; sleepy, sometimes as the result of exposure to a physical or mental stimulus like alcohol.

> *The brandy she drank left her GROGGY; she was so compromised that she felt unable to communicate or try to get home.*

43

H

halfhearted

(*haf-HAHR-tid*)

ADJECTIVE: Without enthusiasm.

hang

(*hang*)

VERB: Slang for spending time in a casual, relaxed manner; as in "hang out."

heavy-eyed

(*HEV-ee-ayed*)

ADJECTIVE: Drowsy, tired; barely able to keep one's eyes open due to exhaustion.

hebetude

(*HEB-ih-tood*)

NOUN: A state of laziness or indolence.

Caught up in the HEBETUDE following the afternoon meal, it was clear no one would move or clean the dishes for several hours.

heedless

(*HEED-lis*)

ADJECTIVE: Uncaring or thoughtless; without regard.

hibernation

(*HY-ber-nay-shuhn*)

NOUN: Though often used in reference to animals, it's a period of time in which a person or animal becomes dormant.

hibernator

(*HY-ber-nay-ter*)

NOUN: One who hibernates.

Indolence is a delightful but

distressing state; we must be

doing something to be happy.

—MAHATMA GANDHI

I

idleness

(*AYED-l-nis*)

NOUN: Unproductiveness; a state of inactivity.

immobility

(*im-oh-BIL-ih-tee*)

NOUN: Not moving; remaining still.

> *She appeared stricken with IMMOBILITY, though it was evident she was able to move freely as she wished.*

impassive

(*im-PAS-iv*)

ADJECTIVE: Emotionless; apathetic; calm.

impervious

(*im-PUR-vee-uhs*)

ADJECTIVE: Not able to penetrate; unaffected; resistant.

impotent

(*IM-puh-tuhnt*)

ADJECTIVE: Lacking strength or ability; the word often used in reference to a man's sexual debility.

improvident

(*im-PROV-i-duhnt*)

ADJECTIVE: Someone who is not sensible, particularly in regard to financial planning for the future.

imprudent

(*im-PROOD-nt*)

ADJECTIVE: Without care of forethought; reckless.

It would be considered IMPRUDENT of you to drive after consuming so much alcohol.

inaction

(*in-AK-shuhn*)

NOUN: Choosing to do nothing when some sort of action is required.

inactivity

(*in-AK-tiv-ah-tee*)

NOUN: A state where something is not active; idleness

inadvertence

(*in-uhd-VUR-tns*)

NOUN: Heedlessness or lack of attention; an oversight.

inane

(*ih-NAYN*)

ADJECTIVE: Senseless or meaningless; absurd.

inanition

(*in-uh-NISH-uhn*)

NOUN: Lack of energy, sometimes in reference to a state of exhaustion as a result of illness or lack of sustenance; lethargy.

inattentive

(*in-uh-TEN-tiv*)

ADJECTIVE: Lacking attentiveness; careless.

inconsequential

(*in-kon-si-KWEN-shuhl*)

ADJECTIVE: Without consequence or importance; insignificant.

> *It was so INCONSEQUENTIAL to him what he ate for dinner that eventually he just stopped ordering altogether.*

incurious

(*in-KYOOR-ee-uhs*)

ADJECTIVE: Lack of curiosity; disinterested.

indifferent

(*in-DIF-er-uhnt*)

ADJECTIVE: Lacking in care of concern; apathetic; uncaring.

indisposition
(*in-dis-puh-ZZISH-uhn*)
NOUN: Disinclination or reluctance.

indolent
(*IN-dl-uhnt*)
ADJECTIVE: Lazy or lethargic; conducive to sluggishness.

ineffective
(*in-ih-FEK-tiv*)
ADJECTIVE: Without results; incompetent.

inept
(*in-NEPT*)
ADJECTIVE: Incompetent; lacking ability or skill.

> *She was completely INEPT at teaching, so she just allowed the students to roam around and find their own lessons.*

inert
(*ih-NURT*)
ADJECTIVE: Lacking the ability to move at all or moving very slowly; motionless.

inexpressive
(*in-ik-SPRES-iv*)
ADJECTIVE: Unable to express oneself; impassive.

ingrate

(*IN-grayt*)

NOUN: Someone who is ungrateful or inconsiderate.

innocuous

(*ih-NOK-yoo-uhs*)

ADJECTIVE: Inoffensive; harmless.

> *Will was so bland and unwilling to get involved in conflict of any sort that everything he said was INNOCUOUS.*

inoperative

(*in-OP-er-uh-tiv*)

ADJECTIVE: No longer operating as it should.

insensate

(*in-SEN-sayt*)

ADJECTIVE: Lacking the ability to feel sympathy or compassion; numb.

insensible

(*in-SEN-suh-buhl*)

ADJECTIVE: Unconscionable; devoid of feeling or sensation.

Far from idleness being the

root of all evil, it is rather the

only true good.

—Søren Kierkegaard

insipid

(*in-SIP-id*)

ADJECTIVE: Uninteresting; dull; the word comes from Latin of "without taste."

insouciance

(*in-SOO-see-uhns*)

NOUN: Indifferent; being without a care in the world.

Her INSOUCIANCE began to wear on him as he realized she would never care as much about anything as he did.

irreligious

(*ir-ih-LIJ-uhs*)

ADJECTIVE: Ungodly; one who does not subscribe to any religious faith or practices.

irresolute

(*ih-REZ-uh-loot*)

ADJECTIVE: Not firm or confident in making commitments or decisions; indecisive.

A person may cause evil

to others not only by his

actions but by his inaction,

and in either case he is

justly accountable to them

for the injury.

—John Stuart Mill

J

jaded

(*JAY-did*)

ADJECTIVE: Bored with something or indifferent toward it because of overexposure or overindulgence.

> *Tired of working long hours with no reward, Sylvie's attitude about her emplyoyer became more and more JADED as the days progressed.*

jejune

(*ji-JOON*)

ADJECTIVE: Immature or unsophisticated; sophomoric.

jelly

(*JEL-ee*)

NOUN: Anything that has a soft, semisolid consistency.

joblessness

(*JOB-lis-nis*)

NOUN: Being without employment.

joyless

(*JOY-lis*)

ADJECTIVE: Without cheer; unhappy.

K

kept

(*kept*)

ADJECTIVE: Maintained and financed by another.

kibosh

(*KAY-bosh*)

NOUN: The act of putting a stop to something or ceasing an activity.

Simon quickly put the KIBOSH on any activity that required him to wake up early.

kick up (one's) feet

(*kik uhp wuhnz feet*)

VERB: To relax.

kip

(*kip*)

NOUN: A British slang term meaning sleep or a place to sleep.

knackered

(*NAK-erd*)

ADJECTIVE: A British slang term meaning extremely exhausted.

He that is busy it tempted by

but one devil; he that is idle,

by a legion.

—THOMAS FULLER

L

lackadaisical

(*lk-uh-DAY-zi-kuhl*)

ADJECTIVE: Lazy; unenthusiastic in one's actions.

lackluster

(*LAK-luhs-ter*)

ADJECTIVE: Uninspiring; dull.

lag

(*lag*)

VERB: To fall behind; the move slower than the rest.

laggard

(*LAG-erd*)

NOUN OR ADJECTIVE: Used as both a noun or adjective in reference to someone who cannot keep up.

laidback

(*layd-BAK*)

ADJECTIVE: Having a carefree disposition; unhurried.

laissez-faire

(*les-ey-FAIR*)

ADJECTIVE: Refraining from interfering in others' business.

> *She was a huge proponent of LAISSEZ-FAIRE parenting; if the children were in need or in trouble, they would figure it out for themselves.*

lallygag

(*LAH-lee-gag*)

VERB: To waste time or loiter, often having fun while doing it.

languidness

(*LANG-gwid*)

NOUN: An unhurried or leisurely manner.

His LANGUIDNESS made him unapologetically late to most social functions.

languor

(*LANG-ger*)

NOUN: Lacking in energy; listlessness, but often in a pleasant way.

lassitude

(*LAS-i-tood*)

NOUN: A state of listlessness or weariness; lethargy.

lax

(*laks*)

ADJECTIVE: Loose and not easily controlled; unmanageable.

layabout

(*LAY-uh-bout*)

NOUN: A lazy or idle person; loafer.

laze

(*layz*)

VERB: To lounge around without worry.

On most days he would LAZE about the house, moving as little as possible before she came home from work.

lazy

(*LAY-zee*)

ADJECTIVE: Reluctant to do work or exert any energy; idle.

lazybones

(*LAY-zee-bohnz*)

NOUN: An idler; someone with a severe lack of ambition.

leaden

(*LED-n*)

ADJECTIVE: Sluggish; immovable; dark or gloomy.

leech

(*leech*)

NOUN: Someone who attaches him or herself to another person in the hope of some sort of personal gain; a bloodsucking worm.

It became apparent that Peter was a LEECH when he stopped working and stayed rent-free in Anna's apartment without contributing to expenses.

Determine never to be idle

... It is wonderful how

much may be done if we are

always doing.

—THOMAS JEFFERSON

leisurely

(*LEE-zher-lee*)

ADJECTIVE: Acting in an unhurried manner.

lethargy

(*LETH-er-jee*)

NOUN: A state of drowsiness or dullness; listlessness.

lie-down

(*LAYE-doun*)

NOUN: A British phrase meaning a nap.

lifeless

(*LAYEF-lis*)

ADJECTIVE: Without life; lacking animation.

limp

(*limp*)

ADJECTIVE: Lacking firmness or energy.

linger

(*LING-ger*)

VERB: To remain in place for longer than would be expected; to hang back.

listless

(*LIST-lis*)

ADJECTIVE: Lethargic; lacking in energy.

loafer

(*LOH-fer*)

NOUN: An idle person; someone who wastes time.

loath

(*lohth*)

ADJECTIVE: Unwilling to or wary of doing something.

> *Ivan was LOATH to do any real work and stood by watching while the rest of the volunteers shoveled snow.*

logy

(*LOH-gee*)

ADJECTIVE: Sluggish and unenthusiastic.

loiter

(*LOY-ter*)

VERB: To waste time or remain in one place without any specific purpose; dally.

loll

(*lol*)

VERB: To recline in a lazy fashion; lounge.

lollygagger

(*LOL-ee-gag-er*)

NOUN: One who loiters or wastes time, often doing something more fun than what he or she should be doing.

looby

(*loo-bee*)

NOUN: An awkward, lazy person; lout.

> *When I called you a LOOBY, it was because you were trying so hard to avoid helping me move this furniture.*

lotus eater

(*LOH-tuhs ee-ter*)

NOUN: From Greek mythology, *lotus eater* has come to describe a daydreamer; someone who doesn't quite live in reality.

lounger

(*LOUN-jer*)

NOUN: A person who behaves in an extremely relaxed manner.

lout

(*lout*)

NOUN: A classless, ill-mannered individual; a hoodlum.

lubber

(*LUHB-er*)

NOUN: An awkward, unintelligent person; looby.

lummox

(*LUHM-uhks*)

NOUN: An unintelligent or dim-witted person.

Leonard was often called a LUMMOX when he was the last to get the joke.

lumpish

(*LUHM-pish*)

ADJECTIVE: Having a heavy, lumplike appearance; devoid of intelligence or vitality.

lusk

(*lusk*)

NOUN: A loafer; idler.

M

malaise

(*ma-LAYZ*)

NOUN: A feeling of worry, lethargy, or mental restlessness.

malingerer

(*muh-LING-gerer*)

NOUN: One who pretends to be sick or injured in order to avoid work.

When Terrence was discovered walking at home without a limp by one of his coworkers, it was clear he was a MALINGERER and should have been back at work weeks ago.

maunder

(*MAWN-der*)

VERB: To ramble or speak in an incoherent manner or mumble; to behave in an aimless fashion.

meander

(*mee-AN-der*)

VERB: To follow an indirect, possibly winding path; to wander in a leisurely way.

meaningless

(*MEE-ning-lis*)

ADJECTIVE: Lacking meaning or purpose; insignificant.

Is sloppiness in speech

caused by ignorance

or apathy?

I don't know and

I don't care.

—WILLIAM SAFIRE

microsleep
(*MAHY-kroh-sleep*)
NOUN: An instance of slumber that happens so quickly, it's barely noticed by the sleeper; it's something often associated with those suffering from narcolepsy or sleep deprivation.

middle-of-the-road
(*MID-l-uhv-thuh-rohd*)
ADJECTIVE: Taking a position in the middle of an argument; not taking sides.

milquetoast
(*MILK-tohst*)
ADJECTIVE: Referencing comic strip character Caspar Milquetoast, someone described as being *milquetoast* is timid and unassertive.

mooch
(*mooch*)
VERB: To sponge off of people with no intention of ever paying them back; as a noun, a *mooch*—or moocher—is the person who does the sponging.

> *Gerry's attempt to MOOCH off of David was thwarted when he realized David had no money to support even himself.*

monotonous

(*muh-NOT-n-uhs*)

ADJECTIVE: Boring or dull; literally, *monotonous* means of one tone.

mope

(*mohp*)

VERB: To sulk or brood; to be apathetic.

mopes

(*mohps*)

NOUN: The doldrums; the blues.

moribund

(*MAWR-uh-buhnd*)

ADJECTIVE: Dying; stagnant.

mosey

(*MOH-zee*)

VERB: To amble along at a leisurely pace; saunter.

> *To ask Barbara to perform any task away from her desk meant watching her MOSEY from one end of the office to the other, taking as much time as possible.*

motionless

(*MOH-shuhn-lis*)

ADJECTIVE: Lacking motion; stationary.

muck about

(*muhk uh-BOUT*)

VERB: To waste time or dally.

mundane

(*muhn-DAYN*)

ADJECTIVE: Common or ordinary; workaday.

> *Going to the theater really has become MUNDANE; it rarely surprises me anymore.*

N

nap
(*nap*)

VERB: To sleep for a short period of time, usually during the day.

narcosis
(*nahr-KOH-sis*)

NOUN: A state of stupor or unconsciousness, often as a result of narcotics.

ne'er-do-well
(*NE-er-doo-wel*)

NOUN: An irresponsible loafer; good-for-nothing.

nebulous
(*NEB-yuh-luhs*)

ADJECTIVE: Something that is vague or confused; cloudy.

> *Asking Grace a question before she was awake meant the answer would be NEBULOUS and nearly impossible to follow.*

neglectful
(*ni-GLEKT-fuhl*)

ADJECTIVE: Careless; forgetful regarding one's duties or responsibilities.

negligent

(*NEG-li-juhnt*)

ADJECTIVE: Acting in a careless, inattentive fashion.

negligible

(*NEG-li-juh-buhl*)

ADJECTIVE: A small, insignificant amount.

nepenthe

(*ni-PEN-thee*)

NOUN: A drug or substance that causes a temporary relief from one's pain or problems.

nescience

(*NESH-ee-uhns*)

NOUN: Lack of knowledge; ignorance.

Your NESCIENCE on the subject is quite appalling, considering how much you are paid to teach it!

neutral

(*NOO-truhl*)

ADJECTIVE: Not favoring any particular side in an argument or dispute; impartial.

Science may have found a

cure for most evils; but it

has found no remedy for

the worst of them all—the

apathy of human beings.

—HELEN KELLER

no-good

(*NOH-good*)

ADJECTIVE: Lacking in positive virtues; worthless.

noctambulist

(*nok-TAM-byuh-liz-uhm*)

NOUN: One who sleepwalks; somnambulist.

Edward was a known NOCTAMBULIST and would sometimes go about his morning routine or prepare a meal while completely asleep.

nodding

(*NOD-ding*)

ADJECTIVE: Something that bends downward; sleepy.

nonchalance

(*non-shuh-LAHNS*)

NOUN: Lack of concern; casualness.

nonentity

(*non-EN-ti-tee*)

NOUN: Someone or thing that is nonexistent or so insignificant that its presence does not matter.

noninterference

(*non-in-ter-FEER-uhns*)

NOUN: Staying out of any part of a dispute, *noninterference* is often used in discussing political matters.

nugatory

(*NOO-guh-tawr-ee*)

ADJECTIVE: Of no value; insignificant.

O

objectless

(*OB-jikt-lis*)

ADJECTIVE: Without an object or purpose; aimless.

oblivion

(*uh-BLIV-ee-uhn*)

NOUN: A state of unawareness or of being completely forgotten.

oblivious

(*uh-BLIV-ee-uhs*)

ADJECTIVE: Unaware of one's surroundings.

obtuse

(*uhb-TOOS*)

ADJECTIVE: Dim-witted; imperceptive; slow to understand.

offish

(*AW-fish*)

ADJECTIVE: Detached; standoffish.

When introduced to new people, Liza was perceived as OFFISH due to her lack of energy or investment into conversation.

ornery

(*AWR-nuh-ree*)

ADJECTIVE: Irritable; obstinate.

Procrastination isn't the

problem, it's the solution.

So procrastinate now,

don't put it off.

—ELLEN DEGENERES

oscitant

(*OS-ih-tuhnt*)

ADJECTIVE: Drowsy; lazy or uninteresting.

otiose

(*OH-shee-ohs*)

ADJECTIVE: Superfluous or not essential; lazy.

So much of our furniture seems OTIOSE; we rarely use any of it.

overtired

(*oh-ver-TY-uhrd*)

ADJECTIVE: Exhausted; overworked.

P

pachydermatous

(*pak-ih-DUR-muh-tuhs*)

ADJECTIVE: Formally, it means having the thick skin or a pachyderm; informally, it refers to someone who is indifferent to criticism.

paralysis

(*puh-RAL-uh-sis*)

NOUN: Complete immobility, voluntarily or otherwise; involuntarily loss of body movement as a result of an injury or some other affliction.

parasite

(*PAR-uh-syt*)

NOUN: Something—including a person—who lives off of another; a sponge or freeloader.

passionless

(*PASH-uhn-lis*)

ADJECTIVE: Without passion or emotion.

passivity

(*pa-SIV-ih-tee*)

NOUN: Submissiveness; obedience.

Her PASSIVITY pleased him; he enjoyed the break from her fighting back.

perfunctory
(*per-FUHNGK-tuh-ree*)

ADJECTIVE: Performed as a matter of routine in a disinterested way; automatic.

phlegmatic
(*fleg-MAT-ik*)

ADJECTIVE: Indifferent or unconcerned; apathetic.

piddle
(*PID-l*)

VERB: To waste time or money; dally.

She hid most of their savings in a can in the pantry; otherwise, he might PIDDLE it away at the racetrack.

pococurante
(*poh-koh-koo-RAN-tee*)

ADJECTIVE: Indifferent or nonchalant; as a noun it is used in reference to someone who is indifferent or uninterested.

plod
(*plod*)

VERB: To move along slowly, as if weighed down by something or not interested in moving ahead. As a noun, it refers to a slow walk or the sound of heavy, lumbering steps.

Know the true value of
time; snatch, seize, and
enjoy every moment of it.
No idleness; no laziness; no
procrastination; never put
off till tomorrow what you
can do today.

—LORD CHESTERFIELD

poky
(*POH-kee*)
ADJECTIVE: Extremely slow; plodding.

poppied
(*POP-eed*)
ADJECTIVE: Behaving in a sleepy manner, as if one has taken an opiate; a more literal translation is to be covered in poppies.

potter
(*POT-er*)
VERB: To move along or complete a task in a leisurely, uninterested manner; to putter.

We would have been finished much sooner if you had chosen to hurry up rather than POTTER about.

procrastinate
(*proh-KRAS-tuh-nayt*)
VERB: To put off doing something until the last possible moment; delay.

profitless
(*PROF-it*)
ADJECTIVE: Without profit or gain.

prosaic

(*proh-ZAY-ik*)

ADJECTIVE: Uninteresting and dull; without any specific features to make it special.

prostrate

(*PROS-trayt*)

ADJECTIVE: Lying in a prone, face-downward position, often as the result of an injury.

As she lay so dramatically PROSTRATE on the bed, she realized everyone was tired of her lazy lifestyle.

purposeless

(*PUR-puhs-lis*)

ADJECTIVE: Without purpose or reason; aimless.

pusillanimous

(*pyoo-suh-LAN-uh-muhs*)

ADJECTIVE: Lacking courage; cowardly.

putrescent

(*pyoo-TRES-uhnt*)

ADJECTIVE: Decaying; rotting.

putter

(*PUHT-er*)

VERB: To *putter* is to move about in a slow, disinterested manner. See *potter.*

Q

quicksand

(*KWIK-sand*)

NOUN: A situation or location where entering is easy and swift but exiting is difficult and tedious.

quiescent

(*kwee-ES-uhnt*)

ADJECTIVE: In an inactive state; resting or dormant.

quietude

(*KWAHY-ih-tood*)

NOUN: A state of quiet, calmness, or tranquility.

As selfish as it sounded, Muriel enjoyed the QUIETUDE while her children were gone to school.

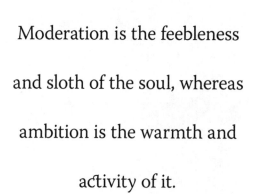

Moderation is the feebleness
and sloth of the soul, whereas
ambition is the warmth and
activity of it.

—François La Rochefoucauld

R

❧

rack out
(*RAK out*)
VERB: To go to sleep.

ramble
(*RAM-buhl*)
NOUN: A stroll or leisurely walk.

recess
(*REE-ses*)
NOUN: A temporary end to activity or labor.

recline
(*ri-KLYN*)
VERB: To lean backward in an attempt to relax.

recumbent
(*ri-KUHM-buhnt*)
ADJECTIVE: Reclining; idle.

> *While lying RECUMBENT on the chaise, Dinah lazily gestured for another glass of wine.*

regardless
(*ri-GAHRD-lis*)
ADJECTIVE: Paying no regard or attention; oblivious.

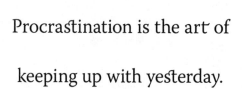

Procrastination is the art of

keeping up with yesterday.

—DON MARQUIS

refrain

(*ri-FRAYN*)

VERB: To hold back or prevent oneself from doing something.

relinquish

(*ri-LING-kwish*)

VERB: To give up or hand something over; to surrender.

remiss

(*ri-MIS*)

ADJECTIVE: Careless; negligent of one's duties.

You would be REMISS to leave your children without first hiring a caregiver.

repose

(*ree-POHZ*)

NOUN: A state of rest or tranquility.

respite

(*RES-pit*)

NOUN: A period of rest; a slight delay.

restful

(*REST-fuhl*)

ADJECTIVE: Allowing for rest; relaxing or tranquil.

resultless
(*ri-ZUHLT-lis*)
ADJECTIVE: Without results; fruitless.

retire
(*ri-TYUHR*)
VERB: To leave the work force permanently; to go to bed. In both cases, the retiree does so in search of relaxation.

> *I shall RETIRE early this evening in hopes of catching more sleep than normal.*

rocker
(*ROK-er*)
NOUN: A chair mounted on two curved pieces that allows one to rock back and forth while sitting.

roly-poly
(*ROH-lee-POH-lee*)
ADJECTIVE: Plump and round.

roost
(*roost*)
VERB: To settle in and rest.

rotund
(*roh-TUHND*)
ADJECTIVE: Round; fat.

rump
(*ruhmp*)
NOUN: Buttocks; backside.

rundown
(*ruhn-DOUN*)
ADJECTIVE: Exhausted or fatigued.

rusty
(*RUHS-tee*)
ADJECTIVE: Out of practice; literally, it also describes something that is covered in rust due to neglect or infrequent use.

The avenues in my neighborhood are Pride, Covetous and Lust; the cross streets are Anger, Gluttony, Envy and Sloth. I live over on Sloth, and the style on our street is to avoid the other thoroughfares.

—JOHN CHANCELLOR

S

sag
(*sag*)
VERB: Droop or wilt; weaken.

sandman
(*SAND-man*)
NOUN: The mythical man who puts sand in your eyes to make you sleepy.

saunter
(*SAWN-ter*)
VERB: To walk along in an unhurried, leisurely manner; meander.

He would SAUNTER through the parties, casually greeting guests without exerting too much energy.

scalawag
(*SKAL-uh-wag*)
NOUN: A dishonest or misbehaved person; rascal.

schlep
(*shlep*)
VERB: To move slowly from one place to the next; to carry something.

scrounger
(*skrounj-er*)
NOUN: One who freeloads or sponges off of others.

sedative

(*SED-uh-tiv*)

ADJECTIVE: Having a calming effect, especially in relation to a drug.

sedentary

(*SED-n-ter-ee*)

ADJECTIVE: Related to the act of sitting; involving little exercise.

> *When Edward stopped doing manual labor and took a more SEDENTARY job, he began slowly gaining weight.*

semiconscious

(*sem-ee-KON-shuhs*)

ADJECTIVE: Existing somewhere between unconsciousness and full consciousness.

senseless

(*SENS-lis*)

ADJECTIVE: Without sensation; lacking perception; meaningless.

shiftless

(*SHIFT-lis*)

ADJECTIVE: Lack of ambition; unwillingness to work in order to be successful.

> *She was an incredibly SHIFTLESS girl; she was trying to get paid without actually doing her job.*

shilly-shally
(*SHIL-ee-shal-ee*)
VERB: To vacillate or be indecisive; to waste time or dawdle.

shirker
(*SHUR-ker*)
NOUN: One who ignores his or her responsibilities; dawdler.

shuteye
(*SHUHT-aye*)
NOUN: Another word for sleep or slumber.

siesta
(*see-ES-tuh*)
NOUN: A nap taken in the early afternoon.

sinecure
(*SAHY-ni-kyoor*)
NOUN: A job that pays well but requires very little work.

skulk
(*skuhlk*)
VERB: To move around in a secret, stealthy manner; as a noun in the U.K. it refers to a shirker, or someone who avoids his or her responsibilities.

slack
(*slak*)
ADJECTIVE: Being loose or relaxed, not taut (as in a rope); lacking in energy or vitality.

slacker
(*slak-er*)
NOUN: One who spends his or her days in an idle manner; malingerer.

> *James was a SLACKER in school and refused to pay attention or do any of his assignments.*

slapdash
(*SLAP-dash*)
ADJECTIVE: Haphazard; disorganized.

sleep-inducing
(*sleep-in-DOOS-ing*)
ADJECTIVE: Something that causes sleep; soporific.

sleepy
(*SLEE-pee*)
ADJECTIVE: Wanting to go to sleep; drowsy.

slipshod

(*SLIP-shod*)

ADJECTIVE: Sloppy; careless; slapdash.

> *The kitchen had a SLIPSHOD appearance; the sink was piled high with dishes, the floor was covered with papers and food, and the oven was open.*

slog

(*slog*)

VERB: Trudge; to work at something for a long time with few results.

slothful

(*SLAWTH-fuhl*)

ADJECTIVE: Lazy; showing a disinclination to work or exertion.

slouch

(*slouch*)

VERB: To stand in a nonupright, drooping fashion; as a noun, a *slouch* is someone who does not care to do something well, a loafer.

> *When you SLOUCH like that, you wrinkle your clothes and ruin your posture.*

slowcoach

(*SLOH-kohch*)

NOUN: Someone who moves very slowly; a laggard.

slowgoing
(*SLOH-GOH-ing*)
ADJECTIVE: Happening at a slow pace.

slowness
(*SLOH-nis*)
NOUN: Characterized by being slow; laggardness.

slowpoke
(*SLOH-pohk*)
NOUN: Someone who moves very slowly; slowcoach.

slug
(*sluhg*)
NOUN: A slow-moving mollusk or a person who behaves in a similarly "sluggish" manner.

slugabed
(*SLUHG-uh-bed*)
NOUN: A person who likes to sleep in past a normal hour.

Henrietta was such a SLUGABED that she would still be sleeping hours after we had all had our breakfast.

sluggard
(*SLUHG-erd*)
NOUN: One who avoids work and other responsibilities.

sluggish
(*SLUHG-ish*)
ADJECTIVE: Slow-moving; lethargic and listless.

slumberland
(*SLUHM-ber-land*)
NOUN: The imaginary place kids are told they visit when they fall asleep.

slumberous
(*SLUHM-ber-uhs*)
ADJECTIVE: Drowsiness; sleepiness.

snooze
(*snooz*)
NOUN: A short nap; used as a verb it means to take a short nap.

somnambulism
(*som-NAM-byuh-liz-uhm*)
NOUN: The technical phrase for sleepwalking; noctambulism.

somniferous
(*som-NIF-er-uhs*)
ADJECTIVE: Having the ability to cause sleepiness.

"I find this conversation SOMNIFEROUS, so I am going to bed," she sighed.

somnolent

(*SOM-nuh-luhnt*)

ADJECTIVE: Drowsy or sleepy; quiet.

soporific

(*sop-uh-RIF-ik*)

ADJECTIVE: Having the ability to cause sleepiness. As a noun, it refers to the thing that causes sleepiness—like a drug.

spiritless

(*SPIR-it-lis*)

ADJECTIVE: Lacking courage or vitality.

sponger

(*SPUHN-jer*)

NOUN: One who lives off of others for all his or her needs; freeloader.

squander

(*SKWON-der*)

VERB: To waste something in an extravagant manner.

He was known to SQUANDER their modest income on elaborate meals and entertainment.

stagnation

(*stag-NAY-shuhn*)

NOUN: A cessation in movement or activity; stasis.

standstill

(*STAND-stil*)

NOUN: A point in time at which all movement and activity stops.

> *The afternoon was at a STANDSTILL as we all were lulled into a heavy sleep with our full bellies.*

stasis

(*STAY-SIS*)

NOUN: A state during which there is no movement, development, or progression; in science, this can be the result of two forces balancing each other out.

static

(*STAT-ik*)

ADJECTIVE: Remaining in a fixed position; stationary.

stationary

(*STAY-shuh-ner-ee*)

ADJECTIVE: To stay in one place; immobile. Not to be confused with stationery, which is the pretty paper upon which you'd write a letter.

Wherever there is

degeneration and apathy,

there also is sexual

perversion, cold depravity,

miscarriage, premature

old age, grumbling youth,

there is a decline in the arts,

indifference to science, and

injustice in all its forms.

—ANTON CHEKHOV

stillness

(*STIL-nis*)

NOUN: Without motion or movement; calmness or tranquility.

stodgy

(*STOJ-ee*)

ADJECTIVE: Devoid of originality; unimaginative and tedious.

stoicism

(*STOH-uh-siz-uhm*)

NOUN: Indifference to all matters—both ones that cause pleasure and those that cause pain.

His STOICISM was amazing; he showed no expression while they debated whether he would live or die.

stolid

(*STOL-id*)

ADJECTIVE: Lacking in emotions; impassive.

stoppage

(*STOP-ij*)

NOUN: A situation where all movement, progress, or work has been stopped.

122

straggler
(*STRAG-ler*)

NOUN: A person who falls behind or wanders off; dawdler.

> *The procession carried on, everyone walking in a straight line, except for one STRAGGLER who had fallen far behind the group.*

stultify
(*STUHL-tuh-fy*)

VERB: To make someone seem unintelligent or foolish.

stupefy
(*STOO-puh-fy*)

VERB: Being unable to think clearly as a result of boredom or tiredness; astonish.

stupor
(*STOO-per*)

NOUN: A trancelike or dazed state, marked by a lack of mental acuteness.

Sloth views the towers of

Fame with envious eyes,

Desirous still,

still impotent to rise.

—WILLIAM SHAKESPEARE

supine

(*soo-PYN*)

ADJECTIVE: Lying on one's back in a face-upward position; remaining totally inactive in a situation that calls for action.

After your surgery it will be necessary for you to remain SUPINE while you recover.

surcease

(*sur-SEES*)

NOUN: Stoppage; intermission.

suspension

(*suh-SPEN-shuhn*)

NOUN: A temporary interruption or stoppage of something, whether it's an employee from his or her post or a student from school.

T

tardiness

(*TAHR-dee-nis*)

NOUN: Lateness; slowness.

tarry

(*TAR-ee*)

VERB: To delay; to linger, especially if in anticipation of something.

> *Don't TARRY as you normally do after dinner because we have so much work to do tonight.*

tedium

(*TEE-dee-uhm*)

NOUN: That which is dull or monotonous.

tentative

(*TEN-tuh-tiv*)

ADJECTIVE: Showing caution or hesitation; allowing for the possibility of changes later on.

tepid

(*TEP-id*)

ADJECTIVE: Lukewarm; halfhearted.

time-wasting

(*tym-WAY-sting*)

ADJECTIVE: Literally, something that wastes time.

It's extraordinary how we

go through life with eyes

half shut, with dull ears,

with dormant thoughts.

Perhaps it's just as well; and

it may be that it is this very

dullness that makes life to

the incalculable majority so

supportable and so welcome.

—JOSEPH CONRAD

toddle

(*TOD-l*)

NOUN: A slow, leisurely walk; stroll.

torpid

(*TAWR-pid*)

ADJECTIVE: Stagnant; lazy; can refer to something that is hibernation or a part of the body that has gone numb.

torpor

(*TAWR-per*)

NOUN: A state of mental and/or physical inactivity.

tractable

(*TRAK-tuh-buhl*)

ADJECTIVE: Easily controlled or manipulated; easy to deal with.

He found that, unlike adults, children were TRACTABLE and easily trained to steal for him.

trail

(*trayl*)

VERB: To walk behind a person or thing; to fall behind or walk in a slow manner as a result of boredom.

traipse
(*trayps*)
VERB: To walk or wander without any specific destination in mind.

trance
(*trans*)
NOUN: A semiconscious or hypnotic state in which some voluntary abilities may be debilitated.

trifling
(*TRY-fling*)
ADJECTIVE: Of little importance; trivial.

trivial
(*TRIV-ee-uhl*)
ADJECTIVE: Unimportant; worthless.

Irene found most conversations TRIVIAL and would not bother to participate in them.

troglodyte
(*TROG-luh-dyt*)
NOUN: Formally, a *troglodyte* refers to an actual cave-dweller during Prehistoric times; informally, it is used to refer to an uncouth, unmannered person or hermit.

Jean-Luc the TROGLODYTE once had excellent manners and social skills, but years of living alone stripped those away.

truant

(*TROO-uhnt*)

ADJECTIVE: Avoiding one's responsibilities without a valid reason; as a noun, it is used in reference to one who shirks his or her duties.

twiddle

(*TWID-l*)

VERB: To fiddle with something; the word is often used in relation to one's fingers.

U

unaffected

(*uhn-uh-FEK-tid*)

ADJECTIVE: Not affected by something in any way; unchanged.

unambitious

(*uhn-am-BISH-uhs*)

ADJECTIVE: Lack of ambition; unmotivated.

unavailing

(*uhn-uh-VAY-ling*)

ADJECTIVE: Not achieving a desired outcome; futile.

unbusied

(*uhn-BIZ-eed*)

ADJECTIVE: Not busy; idle.

> *Because she avoided so many commitments and responsibilities, after a while her days were completely UNBUSIED and empty.*

uncircumspect

(*uhn-SUR-kuhm-spekt*)

ADJECTIVE: Acting without considering the consequences; careless.

unconcern
(*uhn-kuhn-SERN*)
NOUN: A lack of concern or regard; indifference.

uncurious
(*uhn-KYOOR-ee-uhs*)
ADJECTIVE: A lack of curiosity; apathetic.

undemonstrative
(*uhn-duh-MON-struh-tiv*)
ADJECTIVE: Not able to show expression;
impassive.

undesirable
(*uhn-di-ZYUHR-uh-buhl*)
ADJECTIVE: Unwelcome or unwanted; can also be
used as a noun in reference to a person that would
be viewed in that way.

undirected
(*uhn-di-REK-tid*)
ADJECTIVE: Not directed to a specific place or purpose; aimless.

> *Our walk was UNDIRECTED as we wandered the city
> after all the shops were closed.*

undisposed

(*uhn-di-SPOHZD*)

ADJECTIVE: Not prone to do something; unwilling.

Although there were parts of being a father that he enjoyed and eagerly participated in, he was entirely UNDISPOSED to changing diapers.

unemotional

(*uhn-ih-MOH-shuh-nl*)

ADJECTIVE: Without emotion; impassion.

unenergetic

(*uhn-en-er-JET-ik*)

ADJECTIVE: Lacking in energy; lazy.

unexcitable

(*uhn-ik-SY-tuh-buhl*)

ADJECTIVE: Impervious to excitement or enthusiasm; imperturbable.

unexerted

(*uhn-ig-ZURT-ted*)

ADJECTIVE: Without exertion; lacking energy.

The men who create power
make an indispensable
contribution to the Nation's
greatness, but the men
who question power make
a contribution just as
indispensable, especially
when that questioning
is disinterested, for they
determine whether we use
power or power uses us.

—JOHN F. KENNEDY

unfelt
(*uhn-felt*)
ADJECTIVE: Not felt or aware of.

unfruitful
(*uhn-FROOT-fuhl*)
ADJECTIVE: Without success or the desired result; futile.

> *Our efforts to prepare a meal were UNFRUITFUL; maybe if we worked harder or knew how to cook we would be eating right now.*

unindustrious
(*in-DUHS-tree-uhs*)
ADJECTIVE: Lacking in ambition and energy; unproductive.

uninspired
(*uhn-in-SPYUHRD*)
ADJECTIVE: Lacking encouragement or inspiration; bland.

uninterested
(*uhn-IN-ter-uh-stid*)
ADJECTIVE: Showing a total lack of interest; indifferent or apathetic.

unlax

(*uhn-LAKS*)

VERB: A slang term meaning to relax.

unmindfulness

(*uhn-MYND-fuhl*)

NOUN: Unawareness; heedlessness.

unmoved

(*uhn-moovd*)

ADJECTIVE: Not swayed or affected by something; indifferent.

unobservant

(*uhn-uhb-ZUR-vuhnt*)

ADJECTIVE: Not alert or attentive.

> *The UNOBSERVANT mother did not notice when her children slipped outside and ran down the street, returning with candy.*

unoccupied

(*uhn-OK-yuh-pyd*)

ADJECTIVE: Empty or vacant; not currently in use.

unproductive

(*uhn-pruh-DUHK-tiv*)

ADJECTIVE: Producing no significant results; barren.

unresponsive

(*uhn-ri-SPON-siv*)

ADJECTIVE: Not responding or reacting.

unsociable

(*uhn-SOH-shuh-buhl*)

ADJECTIVE: Unfriendly or antisocial; disliking the company of others.

> *The count was UNSOCIABLE; although he didn't mind contributing to charity, he had no desire to attend the fundraising functions or make public appearances.*

unsubstantial

(*uhn-suhb-STAN-shuhl*)

ADJECTIVE: Without substance or strength; worthless.

unsuccessful

(*uhn-suhk-SES-fuhl*)

ADJECTIVE: Not successful; failed.

unthinking

(*uhn-THING-king*)

ADJECTIVE: Not thinking; careless or thoughtless.

unwind

(*uhn-WYND*)

VERB: To relax, particularly after a particularly busy or stressful time.

useless

(*YOOS-lis*)

ADJECTIVE: Of no worthwhile use; ineffective.

V

vacillate

(*VAS-uh-layt*)

VERB: To go back and forth between two sides without making a firm decision.

vacuous

(*VAK-yoo-uhs*)

ADJECTIVE: Empty; unintelligent or dim.

valueless

(*VAL-yoo-lis*)

ADJECTIVE: Of no value; worthless.

vapid

(*VAP-id*)

ADJECTIVE: Lacking any depth; insipid or dull.

She was VAPID and devoid of any real conversation or profound understanding.

vegetate

(*VEJ-i-tayt*)

VERB: To be inactive or sluggish; stagnate.

void

(*voyd*)

ADJECTIVE: To be ineffective or lacking; as a noun it refers to an empty space or loss of something; as a verb it means to cancel or negate.

Iron rusts from disuse;

stagnant water loses its

purity and in cold weather

becomes frozen; even so does

inaction sap the vigor

of the mind.

—LEONARDO DA VINCI

wane
(*wayn*)
VERB: To decrease in power or intensity; to come to an end.

> *He was so used to relaxing rather than working that just a few minutes after picking up a shovel his power would begin to WANE.*

waster
(*way-ster*)
NOUN: A person or thing who wastes something.

wastrel
(*WAY-struhl*)
NOUN: An insulting term coined for those who are wasteful or lazy.

wayward
(*WAY-werd*)
ADJECTIVE: Disobedient or errant; capricious or unpredictable.

weariness
(*WEER-ee-nis*)
NOUN: Tiredness; exhaustion.

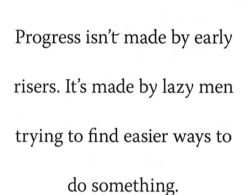

Progress isn't made by early risers. It's made by lazy men trying to find easier ways to do something.

—ROBERT HEINLEN

weltschmerz
(*VELT-shmerts*)
NOUN: In German, *weltschmerz* translates to "world pain" and relates to a certain world-weariness or apathy caused by the current state of affairs in the world.

while away
(*hwyl uh-WAY*)
VERB: To pass time in a leisurely manner.

wither
(*WITH-er*)
VERB: To deteriorate and become weak; shrivel.

>   *Years of avoiding work caused her body to WITHER and become frail.*

woozy
(*WOO-zee*)
ADJECTIVE: Dizzy or faint; confused.

work-shy
(*work-shy*)
ADJECTIVE: Avoiding work or exertion; lazy.

world-weariness

(*wurld-WEER-ee-nis*)

NOUN: Fatigue or boredom with the world and particularly its material things.

worthless

(*WURTH-lis*)

ADJECTIVE: Insignificant or of no value; useless.

Though he volunteered for the cause, he was WORTHLESS when it came to actually helping with the physical labor.

Y and Z

yawn

(*yawn*)

VERB: Involuntarily open one's mouth wide and inhale deeply due to tiredness.

She remained so lazy and tired throughout every day that it was rare for her to go more than a few minutes without a YAWN.

yuppie flu

(*YUHP-ee floo*)

NOUN: An informal term describing any fatigue-causing disorder, like chronic fatigue syndrome, associated with stress.

zone out

(*ZOHN out*)

VERB: To stop paying attention.

zonk

(*zongk*)

VERB: To fall into a deep sleep; to pass out due to intoxication.

Out of passions grow

opinions; mental sloth

lets these rigidify into

convictions.

—Friedrich Nietzsche

DAILY BENDER

Want Some More?

Hit up our humor blog, The Daily Bender, to get your fill of all things funny—be it subversive, odd, offbeat, or just plain mean. The Bender editors are there to get you through the day and on your way to happy hour. Whether we're linking to the latest video that made us laugh or calling out (or bullshit on) whatever's happening, we've got what you need for a good laugh.

If you like our book, you'll love our blog. (And if you hated it, "man up" and tell us why.) Visit The Daily Bender for a shot of humor that'll serve you until the bartender can.

Sign up for our newsletter at
www.adamsmedia.com/blog/humor
and download our Top Ten Maxims No Man Should Live Without.